Third W
Volun

Third Wednesday is a quarterly journal of literary and visual arts. Though we manage the magazine from Michigan, we welcome submissions from all over the world. Digital issues of the magazine are completely free to anyone and print issues can be purchased at Amazon.com.

Find us on the web at **thirdwednesdaymagazine.org** where you can download free digital issues, read the fine poems we have published in the past and find the link to our portal at *Submittable* where you can submit your work and subscribe to the magazine. You can also find us on Facebook, YouTube & Instagram

Masthead

David Jibson, Editor
Laurence W. Thomas, Editor Emeritus
Judith Jacobs, Art Editor
John F. Buckley, Fiction Editor
Dana Louise Johnson, Copy Editor
Marilyn L. Taylor, Associate
Lynn Gilbert, Associate
Carl Fanning, Associate
Phillip Sterling, Associate
Colleen Alles, Fiction Contest Judge

Cover Art:
Puerto Penasco—Photograph
Soleil Ponce / Ann Arbor, Michigan

Editor's note for Fall 2025..4
Weathered Tree on Ocotillo Trail, Phoenix / Michael C. Roberts......5
For Every Wedding / Ron Koertge...6
Forget / Meighan Sharp...7
Swift / Meighan Sharp...8
Where Did I Put Them? / Yakov Azriel..9
Early Winter / Ginel Ople..10
Heirloom / Catherine Kennedy..11
Cuts / Catherine Kennedy..12
Kindness Toward My Other Self / Horia Pop......................................13
Another Life / Michael Minassian..14
The Glove / Michael Minassian...15
Morning Prayer / Kenneth Pobo..16
A Kiss To Build a Dream On / Kathy O'Fallon...................................17
Pray for the Cardinals Today / A. J. Saur..18
Child's Play / Gary Wadley...19
Taino Face in Stone / Roxanne Cardona..20
A Better Sadness / Noah Berlatsky..21
When a Tulip Poplar Sends a "Friend" Request / Gene Hyde.........22
Inscription / Brett Warren..23
Seven Years After My Husband Dodged Death / Jessica Dubey......24
I Don't Mind / Randy Streu..25
A Dead Letter / Thomas Cullen..26
Looking Down / Sabahat Ali Wani..27
On The Most Comfortable Shoes On Planet Earth / Lily Tobias.....28
On My Brother's Bedroom / Lily Tobias..28
Origami / Dolores Diaz...29
Our Sun / Robert Kinerk..30
Mirror / Aaron Hicks..31
Six Years of Becoming / Michal Mendelsohn..32
For the Last Time / Bridget Brush...34
Extremely Rare but Serious Side Effects / Paul Hostovsky...............35
Song for Bill / Paul Hostovsky..36
Yes / Emily Zhang...37
The Cane's on Fire / Evrard Klein..38
Octavio / David Chorlton...39
Monsoon Local Time / David Chorlton..40
The Minutes / Gloria Parker..41
Sometimes My Thoughts Remind Me / Robert Fillman.....................42
Still Life with Mother and Son / Stan Hodson......................................43
Soap Operas and Sandboxes / Annette Sisson......................................44
Library 2 / Lisa Yount...45

The Hourglass and the Sea / Lucien R. Starchild..............................46
When the Time Comes / Leslie Schultz...47
George Dila Memorial Flash Fiction Contest....................................48
   Dressed to Krill / Sigrun Benjamin...50
   Blue Fever / John Spudich..54
   Moirologist / Colleen Addison...56
   Off the Menu / JR Walsh..57
   Reading Tea Leaves / Elyse Ribbons..60
   Hit Me With Your Best Shot / Nan Jackson......................................61
   A Queen Anne Treasure / Kimberly Hayes......................................63
Lifted / Emily Zhang..67

Editor's note for Fall 2025

This issue marks the seventh year for our annual George Dila Memorial Fiction Contest honoring the memory of George Dila, friend of Third Wednesday and the editor who originally brought fiction to 3W. We are proud to have called him friend and colleague.

This year's contest judge is Colleen Alles. Colleen is a writer, former librarian & teacher, and Michigan girl for life. She earned her bachelor's degree in English from Michigan State University and her MLIS from Wayne State University. Her fiction and poetry have appeared in Red Cedar Review, Tar River Poetry, The Write Michigan Anthology, The Michigan Poet, and other places. Her fiction has been longlisted for The Fugere Book Prize for Finely Crafted Novellas in 2023 (Regal House Publishing). Colleen is co-editor for fiction with Barren Magazine and is currently pursuing her MFA at Spalding University.

In addition to the winning and honorable mention stories published in these pages, there is also a special chapbook of just those stories in downloadable form at our website.

Not to be overlooked, there is also a lot of fine poetry and artwork in this issue, including work from old friends and new. So lets get on with it. You've got a lot of reading ahead of you.

Weathered Tree on Ocotillo Trail, Phoenix / Michael C. Roberts

Photograph
Michael C. Roberts / Anthem, Arizona

For Every Wedding / Ron Koertge

there's another wedding where
the bride says, "Death is preferable
to a loss of virtue."

A friend of mine saved that line
for her honeymoon but her
husband didn't

think it was funny. He was
on a regular honeymoon featuring
a heart-shaped bed.

She was on the other honeymoon,
Where there's no cake, no Brut
champagne.

Yet all the animals line up to put their
mangy heads in her lap.

    Ron Koertge / South Pasadena, California

Forget / Meighan Sharp

Give up the alley's exit to the yard, the sneaking
snap of lemon, last sugar of summer, lessons
memorized like vinyl's lyric columns, played
and replayed, the minor lift and drop of arms,
the vacant space between tracks, the places
we hesitate as if waiting will return to us
the music of gravel and garbage, the pause
of August's cracked passages. Give up
the biting edges of fences, the trip of clothes
caught on splintered wood, our sideways turns,
bent nails catching our backs, those divot scars
evidence of memory, evidence of night's
exuberant structure, light dissolving
and returning, trying one more time to tell us
                    we must all give up
love's well-lit pools, love's ill-lit halls,
those shimmered conversations
we tended like tender flames.

    Meighan Sharp / Roanoke, Virginia

Swift / Meighan Sharp

Tuesday, you opened the flue and fifty swifts
swooned through—out the front door—
cautious and exhausted, their sky dives
patterning twilight. Your mother had just died.
She wanted a moment to sit on the stoop before
leaving, a view of the smoke-shrouded sunset
crowding the mountains. She wanted to pause
in the evening that had been her life. Fifty swifts
crested her head, called to her—stranger, they said,
give us your hands. And though you reached again for her,
though you reached—
> the swifts' sky was blackberry, half-ripe, and her hands
> rose and opened, moonflowers to their night.

Meighan Sharp / Roanoke, Virginia

Where Did I Put Them? / Yakov Azriel

Where did I put them?   Scissors. Watches. Locks.
My leather wallet. Pillow cases. Bread
to feed the pigeons, though I might have fed
them earlier today. Where is the box
my daughter treasured, filled with pretty rocks
she stored inside? Where is the little bed
on which she put her dolls to sleep? And thread
for sewing all the holes in threadbare socks?

Where did I put the ceiling and the floor?
Where did I put Miss Muffet and her curds
and whey, her spider and her spider's cage?
Where did I put the window and the door?
The door is bolted, the window—shut. And words
which used to glow have fallen off the page.

   Yakov Azriel / Jerusalem, Israel

Early Winter / Ginel Ople

While friends and lovers waited
in the backrooms of my distant future,
I stood on my parents' balcony
having my first ever beer alone.

I was sent home from choir practice
for calling Mary Kate a nun
when I didn't have the nerves
to say that I loved her. She would never

know about it now. The hunters
chasing deer in the mountains,
they had no idea I was listening.
Their rifles echoed

through the still air of the woods,
over the chapel where the other kids
were angels singing Benedictus
and to our little house where,

as the sun began to hold its breath,
the first snowflake in Minnesota
drifted onto a parapet to give me
this memory that is only mine.

    Ginel Ople / Cavite, Phillipines

Heirloom / Catherine Kennedy

He pulled a carrot from his garden
like a bookmark from the pages of earth,
straight up from the neat lines of bushy
greens, which he read like a fable,
left to right, as he handed it
to me, a child,
this gift.

What does a young girl know
of her grandfather besides the translation
of his presence into feeling? I held the carrot
in my hands until the stem and leaves wilted,
until the root grew soft like an eraser.
I relished the feeling scribbled
down my spine—

Delight, as good an epithet as any
for a story of seed and soil, sun and rain
with the divine power to transfigure earth's deep
and epic darkness, to deliver love without
even the word for love, to endow
the only relic a child need
ever to inherit.

    Catherine Kennedy / Columbus, Ohio

Cuts / Catherine Kennedy

Wouldn't you know—the branches that gather
across the kitchen windows have finally been forced
to give up their secret as the ground has softened,
and the sun and spotty rains have teased out the leaves
along their many twiggy tines. It must have been
in the dreary offices of dormancy that hard decisions
were made about budgets and funding cuts,
but we didn't hear one word, and now it's clear
which branches weren't renewed for another season,
are now exposed, shamefully bare from stock to stem.
I will have to trim them out, I suppose, and shouldn't
we all? Take time, that is, to remove the dead wood
from the living? It's hard enough to thrive
without holding on to what simply isn't serving,
so darn hard to draw from what little else
any one of us has left to give.

    Catherine Kennedy / Columbus, Ohio

Kindness Toward My Other Self / Horia Pop

Photograph
Horia Pop / Salon de Provence, France

Another Life / Michael Minassian

How long will you hold suffering
in your mouth, or cling to memories

of whiskey days and nights,
sweat drenched motels on the edge

of a desert town somewhere
in Arizona or New Mexico

where borders are black lines on a map,
blown across the highway by the wind.

I remember a dusty road, cactus blooms,
a chenille bedspread, pink and green,

a busted ice machine, the last joint
we shared, bought from a Navajo

at the bus station, how the stars
seemed to pinwheel behind our eyes

and we heard coyotes yipping
in the hills, then took up our own howl,

dissolved into laughter so hard you peed
yourself, and I snorted beer through my nose.

Years later when I saw you
in the parking lot of a Winn-Dixie

in Clearwater, Florida, you still
held your anger like a thorn

under the skin, the way you spit
out my name before slamming

the car door and drove off,
a part of me still in the desert,

my teeth and tongue, dry sockets,
sand, wind, and dark clouds,

the threat of rain, a sound like bad
dreams beating on rooftops.

The Glove / Michael Minassian

After the divorce
from my first wife,
after she left
with her brother
for the long drive
back to California
to the family
that had ruined her,
I cleaned out the closet
and found an old t-shirt,
a pair of her boots,
and a single glove,
too small to fit,
though I squeezed
my fingers in
to feel her hand
from the inside:
the fist she made,
the last message
she left behind.

    Michael Minassian / Providence, Rhode Island

Morning Prayer / Kenneth Pobo

We stand while Pastor
gives the morning prayer.
After Our Father I count down
in order the Top 10 songs
on WCFL, hope the ice cream
truck will roll by once church
is over. It never has,
but maybe today?
In summer I think of the Yankees,
fear a loss more than an
angry God. The God pastor
prays to is often out of sorts.
Then there's school, some
geometry problem that
I'll have to put on the board,
wrong from the first step.

I know church will end soon
as he's praying for our leaders.
He means Republican leaders.
How happy to sit again
after the Amen, pretend
I'm on a deep-cushioned couch,
not a wooden pew.

    Kenneth Pobo / Media, Pennsylvania

A Kiss To Build a Dream On / Kathy O'Fallon

Song sung by Louis Armstrong

We climb out our bedroom window just over the garage, my bed lined up
conveniently under the opening. Sit down, I say to my sister, who wants to

twirl along the roof-line like a ballerina in pajamas. She's five, and at seven,
I'd be in big trouble if she splatted onto the yard, where our parents are hosting

a party for the only time I can recall, after we've all been kissed in bed,
though Tommy's probably figuring out how to escape his crib.

I've ventured out before, spying on the boy next door whose window
faces mine above a screened-in porch, while he studies at his desk—

dark-haired and tall, athletic like my father. Once he sneaked a smoke
on the flat roof and said hi, as if he'd known all along I'd been watching.

I almost died, couldn't wait until he did it again. But a few years from now,
after we've talked about the future—his plans for college, us moving

to a bigger house soon (more babies born each year)—he gets drafted,
and never makes it home from Vietnam.

But tonight I don't yet know the crushing weight of loss, and as the cocktails empty,
my father returns them full, though not himself a drinker until wife number two.

And though the deviled eggs get soggy and the celery sticks look lonely under stars
erased by clouds, fireflies like fairies wave infinity signs between the oaks,

and friends we hardly know start swaying to Satchmo—the E major trumpet,
the gravelly hypnotic hum—cigarette smoke turning it all into a movie.

Soon the mosquitoes will have had their fill and the guests will usher
themselves home by flashlight, but my sister's yawns can't wait that long,

so back in bed we go, drift off to the surprising rise of laughter,
and dreams I won't recall.

Kathy O'Fallon / Carlsbad, California

Eds Note: Small print is due to long lines.

Pray for the Cardinals Today / A. J. Saur

~Request on the death of Pope Francis

But what of the blue jays and orioles
or those red-bereted Sandhill cranes arriving
all at once along the Platte River on their way north?

See how they bow their heads
for minnows and the sun-crazed frogs
emerging from hibernation. We are consumed

by our binoculars as they fold
and unfold their massive wings and progress
their knobby knees in a liturgy

only the most ardent follow.
But none of us take on faith
what can be captured on camera—

the collective slanting of necks seeking
spring's first insects. There is no count
of the days we are sequestered there

while downstream the dead grass and leaf
litter of the DNR's controlled burn transforms
into white smoke—the will of man

made evident, announced on winds
momentarily seen, but long known by greater
(and lesser) birds taking flight.

    A. J. Saur / Grand Rapids, Michigan

Child's Play / Gary Wadley

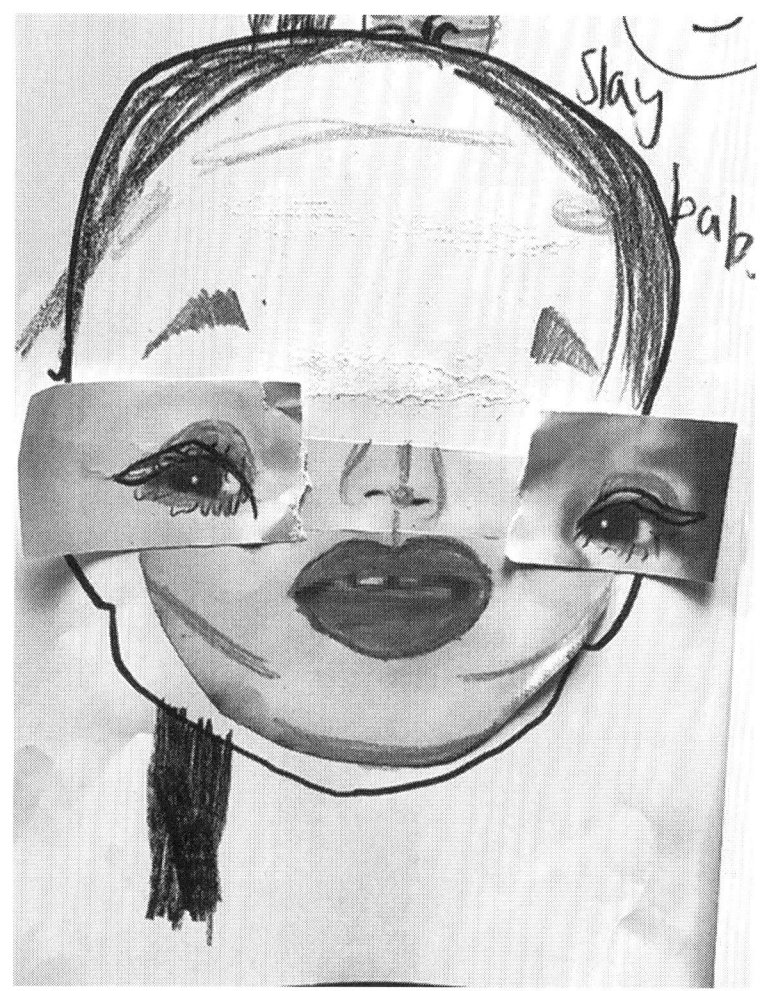

Collage
Gary Wadley / Louisville, Kentucky

Taino Face in Stone / Roxanne Cardona

after illustrations by Rafael Tufiño

Trapped on a page from an old cookbook,
a Taino God, his face drawn

in charcoal, once carved
in stone. A startle of eyes,

black as a raven's feather
stare at me, a relic

of those salted centuries
marked by wind storms. Amidst

the recipes for coconut bread pudding
and sweet guava jelly,

I think of his captivity, inside this book. Those eyes
that do not grieve.

Two lids missed, that are missing
perhaps a misplaced idea,

a totem erased. The recipe I sought, now
incidental, as his face peers

into mine, perplexed. Both of us startle.
Atop his skull, a single feather waves

like a cicatrix. Double loops for ears appear
on either side of his masked face.

Pebbles seem to drop from his mouth—
small oracles of a future

neither one of us can decipher.
I must decide which recipe to follow—

one contains French bread, crust trimmed
the other guava— both sweet and sour.

    Roxanne Cardona / Teaneck, New Jersey

A Better Sadness / Noah Berlatsky

Imagine a billionaire.
He is sad.
So he drowns the world in something disgusting.
Mayonnaise jello, maybe.
Or antisemitism.
It doesn't matter.
The point is that he does it because he is sad.
And if he were not sad
he would maybe not be a billionaire.
That's the poetry of it.
And while you choke on lead paint
or misogyny
remember that at least you're not sad
like billionaires. Your sadness
produces nothing and has no narrative value.
Take comfort.

    Noah Berlatsky / Chicago, Illinois

When a Tulip Poplar Sends a "Friend" Request / Gene Hyde

I didn't see this coming, that
upstart sapling reaching out to
me while I sit on my deck, binge
watching the woods every day.
But, really, there's a comfort in
knowing there's a Wood Wide Web,
trees in the ultimate social network,
taking all shock and woe in stride,
repairing itself, in time. Saplings
rise, children destined to age with
their friends into a canopy, light from
the sky doing that magic thing,
chlorophyll the green miracle,
all plugged in and growing. Decades
from now the hill will be healed.
So, yeah, befriend that tulip poplar,
plug in like the world was connected
underground, root by root, undaunted
by any mischief we can muster.

   Gene Hyde / Asheville, North Carolina

Inscription / Brett Warren

After the reading, a woman approaches
and asks me to inscribe my book for a friend
with terminal cancer.

Another author murmurs, *Good luck
with that,* and I briefly consider cribbing
what she said. But humor can be tricky,

interpretation a wilderness, so I go
with the more direct, *May you find poetry
everywhere.*

Driving home, I think about the everywhere,
hope it will be there, complete and constant,
for the woman with cancer. I wish I'd added

I hope you go on.

I don't know why these words come to mind,
since *going on* can mean living or dying or both.
This is the trouble with words—every shimmer

is also a blur. My car barrels along, bog
on one side, forest on the other. I reach
the darkest stretch of road, where one night

last year, a coyote ran across, wildly alive, full
of intention. I feared for him, even as I wanted
to be him, disappearing into rushes and reeds.

I switch my high-beams on, slow down,
scan the edges for eyes reflecting.
I make it home without anyone dying.

    Brett Warren / Yarmouth Port, Massachusetts

Seven Years After My Husband Dodged Death / Jessica Dubey

Thunder slaps the sky. It leaves no bruise,
the canopy above us already black and blue
with the charged night. With the next blow
the storm comes closer—one-one-thousand,
two-one-thousand, three, four, five seconds
from flash to boom. The next bolt has teeth.
I hold my breath. How often do we get
such a clear warning of what comes next?
The dog presses against me, her trembling
creates a circuit from her body to mine.
My husband chooses this moment
to take a shower as if he doesn't know
how water and electricity taunt each other,
so captivated by the chaos of their union.
He won't wait until the storm
has passed, until the water is just water.
What is it that makes him fill
the chamber and spin to see if disaster
will strike again? His body so recently
made whole. He seems to forget
how fast fate travels, so target hungry
it makes a bullet seem ambivalent.

    Jessica Dubey / Endicott, New York

I Don't Mind / Randy Streu

(for my children)

I don't mind
late-night pickups,
or early mornings
pre-coffee.

I don't mind
five-hour drives
or coordinating schedules
to fit it all in,
working in the here-and-there
hours that remain.

I don't mind
windows down,
rain on the windshield,
noise of the traffic,
or the driver's Chess of changing lanes.

I don't mind--
just so we can spend the time
and you say you love me
when you leave the car

Randy Streu / Appleton, Wisconsin

A Dead Letter / Thomas Cullen

There is a letter that arrived yesterday.
A linen white envelope that has turned
yellow around the edges, mailed in May
post marked decades ago. I learned

pain can find you anywhere. When it came
her beautiful sprawling script drifting
across the envelope, like waves. - The same
swirls and rushes, the beach shifting

the sands around our toes those many years ago.
The letter is a relic, sent to a person who
no longer exists. A message out of time, too slow -
written long ago before we knew

the swirling rushing waves would erase
all trace of our sad quick short embrace.

    Thomas Cullen / Madison, Wisconsin

Looking Down / Sabahat Ali Wani

Photograph
Sabahat Ali Wani / Budgam, Kashmir, India

On The Most Comfortable Shoes On Planet Earth / Lily Tobias

I am looking for shoes with orthotics of cloud
that forgive like God. I am looking
for a lace-less variety, something easy to slip
on and off. I am looking for halos for my toes.
I am looking for soles that take on the arch
and curve of my own. I am not asking for much.
I believe such shoes exist.

On My Brother's Bedroom / Lily Tobias

Here is an ancient wisdom, here is a woman in a gold bikini
forever with her hands on her hips, here is the CD I stole,
here is an unopened book. Here is a reason for mutiny,
here is a curtain drawn. Here is a cup half empty.
Here is a sketchbook, the same image over and over.
Here is a weapon. Here is a relic, the baoding balls I held
in silence after creeping inside. Here is my brother still alive.

    Lily Tobias / Auburn Hills, Michigan

Origami / Dolores Diaz

You wear that worn-out blue suit,
the old pain wears you.
It bends your tall body
like an oak, young bones
ancient and knotted, branches
contorting, eager for sunlight.
Your eyes retreat more and more,
and no longer meet mine.
Inwards is the North.
You fold and fold and fold
like origami, longing for beauty
in the folds but finding more
and more pain. A pain that

was scored and creased
into you from the beginning.
A pain that also
folds into me.

    Dolores Diaz / Palo Alto, California

Our Sun / Robert Kinerk

is the star with the smiley face
children show us in their drawings
until the thought occurs to them
there is no smile like a happy face
pasted across the sun's great ball of fire.
Out comes the eraser. Away goes the grin.

Which has no effect on the star we call ours,
but our star is one of trillions,
and in galaxies unknown to us,
too far away for telescopes to see,
there might be stars wearing smiley faces,
and every time that eraser does its work
one of those blinks out.

Children have no agency in this.
They're doomed to learning dumb reality
and thinking dumb reality is all they need to know.
Science intervenes.
Swift erasures occur.

And suddenly a star
somewhere no one knows,
suddenly that star
goes dark.

    Robert Kinerk / Cambridge, Massachusetts

Mirror / Aaron Hicks

When I look into her face,
I see my own—
a mirror softened by time.
Every gray hair,
every fold of loosened skin
marks the quiet touch of time—
its hands resting gently on our shoulders,
guiding us forward.
In the tender lines of my mother's face,
each wrinkle speaks—
a word etched deep,
a sentence formed across years.
Her face tells our story,
moving steadily
word by word,
page by page.
Her sweet face remains
the color of oolong tea,
held in a cup still half full—
warm, steeped in memory.
And now, silver strands rise like dawn,
a luminous crown
gracing her brow.
She wears it well—
a testament to beauty shaped by years,
to a life endured and embraced,
adorned in quiet resilience,
wrapped in the wisdom of time.

Aaron Hicks / Columbia, South Carolina

Six Years of Becoming / Michal Mendelsohn

In the beginning,
I was a woman with rooms inside--
each one filled with voice, color,
echoes of my own name.

Then he needed me,
all the time,
all the way through--
not just love,
but vigilance,
a fierce devotion with no clocking out.

Days folded into each other.
I began to speak in whispers,
or not at all.
My reflection blurred;
I became outline instead of form.

Grief came slowly--
not a storm,
but fog seeping under every door.
He was still here,
but already half-not.
I wept for him while still feeding him,
held a hand that forgot mine.

Now--
he is gone.
And I live
as though I'm not quite sure
what "living" means anymore.
The silence is loud,
the bed too large;
the hours impossibly long,
even as they slip by unnoticed.

I shrink from gatherings,
not because I don't want company,
but because I no longer know
how to be with others
without feeling the hole beside me.

Loneliness isn't new--
but age sharpens its edges.
And sometimes,
I forget who I was before
the world became caretaking and grief.
Yet--
somewhere under the ache,
there is still breath.
Still time.
Still a sliver of self
quietly calling me back.

I don't know the "her" anymore,
but I think
she's waiting.

  Michal Mendelsohn / Naperville, Illinois

For the Last Time / Bridget Brush
From last pictures of homes taken before evacuations.

Before we left for the last time he closed
the cabinets. Gently, like he does everything else, he emptied
the dishwasher, stacked plates and bowls and placed cups alternating
which way the rim was facing. He says he fits more that way. His
    socked feet silent
on the wood floors of our apartment. Silent. He usually likes music,
I would have liked music. Stop the tears as they roll down my
    cheeks, pack up
our clothes, his mothers old quilt, the entire set of pictures lining our
    hallway. Leave
the couch and the TV but pack up my jewelry and his great
    grandfather's watch. Leave
the expensive things, take the priceless ones. We don't want this. To
    go, to leave,
to run, but we don't want to die. Check every corner of the
    apartment, still only in socks,
scan the cabinets he closed so gently, the empty closets and drawers,
triple check. He puts on his shoes and checks one more time, I'll put
    on mine and follow
taking pictures. It's not silent anymore, the sounds of rubber soles
    echo
around what's left. The couch the tv, the expensive things. The
    priceless ones
in boxes and suitcases by the door. It probably won't matter how
    gently he closed
the cabinets, or how the dishes were stacked. I know how this place
    trembles
I hear the rattling bones of this building the way it shakes
when the neighbors kids wrestle and slam doors. It feels like a
    dream,
the whole place looks different. Maybe it is and I am
seeing it for the last time. Silent
for the first time.

    Bridget Brush / Salisbury, Maryland

Extremely Rare but Serious Side Effects / Paul Hostovsky

including death have been reported—
not that death is rare, death is commonplace,

an everyday occurrence. Everyone and everything
dies. Even the sun will die and the stars—
many of them—are dead already.

"If I knew that dying was going to be this easy,
I would have done it long ago," he said. He was being

serious and also funny. Maybe he was taking medication
that put him in a jokey mood on his deathbed,

his loved ones gathered round, wringing their hands
and crying, because it was all so serious.

Until he said that. He said it to no one
in particular. No one laughed at first. Then

someone did. Then suddenly they were all laughing
and feeling almost good about dying, which was
neither as serious nor as rare as had been reported.

    Paul Hostovsky / Medfield, Massachusetts

Song for Bill / Paul Hostovsky

That was a lovely death.
Quick and clean and painless,
dying in your sleep like that
just five days after stopping
dialysis. Just two months after
deciding to do it. Time enough
to max out your credit cards,
sell all your stuff, give all the money
to your daughter who doesn't
have any money. I bought the 5-
string banjo, the wooden stool,
two hanging plants, the framed
calligraphed Whitman quote
about going freely with powerful
uneducated persons. And the clutch
of harmonicas. You told me
I better wash them because
"they probably still have my spit in them."
I haven't washed them. I hold one
up to my mouth, put my tongue
to the wooden holes. Inhale.
Exhale. Lovely. Lovely.

    Paul Hostovsky / Medfield, Massachusetts

Yes / Emily Zhang

Charcoal Drawing
Emily Zhang / Bellevue, Washington

The Cane's on Fire / Evrard Klein

They call this town Big Bend because of the river.
The Usuthu makes a big bend here before it
rushes to the Indian ocean. I'm sitting at the foot
of a tall palm tree, having made sure it bore
no cluster that would likely split my skull if it fell.
The wind is rustling through the wide pinnate leaves.

From the hilltop where the hotel stands, I overlook the valley.
The earth's red clay forms a checkerboard
on the ground as it alternates with the green sugarcane fields.
The golden sunlight is slowly abating, leaving
way to a red dusky glow. In the distance,
volutes of smoke rise from the fiery fields.
The cane is set alight before harvest.
One fire dies, another flares up.
The shades of ruby and emerald are unmistakable.

On the other side of the valley, the Lubombo plateau
marks the invisible border. Borders are invisible.
In Zulu, Lubombo means forehead. Fitting, for a ridge.
I turn mine: peacocks are courting at the edge
of the pool, oblivious of the view and of the rising wind.
Increasing gusts shake the palm trees and ruffle
the pages of my notebook, urging me to seek shelter.
But I do nothing of the sort. I'll stay and watch.
I wouldn't miss this show for the world.

    Evrard Klein / Champigny sur Marne, France

Octavio / David Chorlton

He's a thimbleful of jaguar mixed
with centuries of house cat.
Wears sleep as a disguise
suggesting domesticity, but once the clock
between his eyes ticks daylight
he wants and wants.
Sunlight on the mountain,

kibble in his dish, white bread
on the table, he'll eat
anybody's breakfast when the window
blinds are raised. Postprandially resting
with finches in focus

he adjusts the flow of his spine
and leaps to where their feeder hangs
on the safer side of glass.
Race from wall to wall, complain enough
is not enough by chewing
magazines as though they grew in jungles
and investigate

any open drawer or door to where
he's not allowed. Breakages
are part of his identity, the collateral damage
of being alive. He must
be dreaming when he's curled into a question
mark of fur, must remember

the unrecorded months
before unsheathing his claws to snag
each passing day as though
time were meant to bleed.

Monsoon Local Time / David Chorlton

First taste of a storm
on the lips of the moon, wind
roaming lost in the foothills and midnight
holds its breath. Tomorrow's news
rumbles in the distance
while music from the borderlands plays on
a radio tuned to dreams. The kitchen clock

says rain is due, the headlines in the clouds
won't commit to moisture
or to justice. Darkness breaking open,
secrets in all directions, thunder beats
on Heaven's door, hummingbirds asleep,
and hawks nesting close to the sky

keep one eye open
to be ready
when the first drop falls.

    David Chorlton / Phoenix, Arizona

The Minutes / Gloria Parker

At the yearly Conference of Celestial Canines,
we meet to discuss what's been going on below.

We were deeply saddened that many of our own
became casualties of war, but were heartened

by the knowledge that not a single dog
played a role in the creation of those conflicts.

California was struck by devastating wildfires
Many dogs perished, but not one was suspected
of arson.

We read the statistics on poverty and pollution
and began to discuss the daily bouts of insanity
in the political arena,

but had to cut it short, as so many in attendance
couldn't stop themselves from howling at the moon.

We can't help it...we get our hopes up...seems it's
the nature of the beast, but year after year ends
with a whimper.

We have to keep reminding each other that we did
the best we could, though admittedly, as a species,
we did find it difficult to bite the hands that feed us.

But even with that, there's still no denying
it's a people-eat-people world down there.

    Gloria Parker / Wayne, Pennsylvania

Sometimes My Thoughts Remind Me / Robert Fillman

of flightless birds. They're too big
for their own good and clumsy

to look at. Always tethered
to the earth, not dinosaurs

exactly but almost as
scary. Their disposition

is to run, to claw at things,
to stab a beak in the soft

underbelly of problems
and peck, or strip the matter

off the nearest low-hanging
branch. They can be aggressive

and territorial. They
could be on the winding road

toward extinction. Would they
get there faster if they flew?

Someone else's thoughts might soar
into powerlines or crash

into sliding glass doors, stunned
that they've fallen from the sky,

while mine just wobble about,
beings that defy logic.

    Robert Fillman / Macungie, Pennsylvania

Still Life with Mother and Son / Stan Hodson

    for Mary Cassatt

The little boy cannot sleep, he has the croup.
His mother is up with his cough,
To run the vaporizer and to keep
Him company. They leave the lights off
For the rest of the family. The front rooms
Are lit by the corner streetlight,
The back rooms by moonlight on snow.
The boy has no schedule to keep tomorrow.
In his life the hour is not early, not late.
It's just the middle of night.

If you ask him his address, he can recite one
But since this is the only house he's known
He doesn't yet have an address.
If you ask him his age, he will say a number.
But since he's still coming to in his own
Life, he doesn't know that he is born.
The young person who is his
Mother has always been
There. Like the streetlight, the moon,
The snow, the breathing house.

    Stan Hodson / Bellingham, Washington

Soap Operas and Sandboxes / Annette Sisson

> As the World Turns aired on CBS from
> April 2, 1956, to September 17, 2010.
> —Wikipedia

Afternoons, our neighbor in the duplex
next door pressed blouses, her daughters'

dresses, husband's shirts. A Coke bottle
sweated on the wide end of the ironing board,

cigarette butts angled in a sea of ash,
the soap's storyline a slow leak in a slick

bathtub. Scenes whirled across the fluorescent
screen like the globe I spun into a frenzy

of countries, borders blurring. My mother
never smoked or watched soaps, nor drank

Cokes except on Friday nights when she fried
burgers, sliced potatoes into scorching oil.

Yet the two of them, one wearing kitten heels,
the other flats, confided at the kitchen table,

lingered, curtains rustling the open window.
This friend packed my lunch, helped me

choose my first pair of penny loafers
while Mom languished in the hospital, cancer

gnawing her kidney, somehow the earth still
rolling through space. I doubt these women

voted for the same president, or even governor,
but their children shared a giant sandbox spanning

the unmarked property line. Together the kids
molded towers, constructed whole towns until dusk.

   Annette Sisson / Brentwood, Tennessee

Library 2 / Lisa Yount

Digital Collage

Lisa Yount / El Cerrito, California

The Hourglass and the Sea / Lucien R. Starchild

I held time once—not in my hands,
But in the hollow of my throat,
A slow dissolve of salted sands,
Each grain a word I could not quote.

The tide, indifferent, dragged its lace
Across the ribs of broken ships,
While I, a beggar for its grace,
Counted the waves with trembling lips.

What is a shore but a farewell
That never learns to close the door?
The sea will rise, the sea will swell,
And leave its wreckage on the floor.

Yet something in the driftwood's curve
Still hums of forests, green and tall.
As if the world forgets to starve,
As if the tide could pardon all.

And so I wait, half-silt, half spark,
For waves to rewrite what they stole,
Not for the moon to mark the dark,
But for the dark to mend the whole.

    Lucien R. Starchild / Fort Lauderdale, Florida

When the Time Comes / Leslie Schultz

I hope to remember
to perform the right action—
to scatter forget-me-not seeds
on newly silvered earth
before the first steel-hard frost;

to light the beeswax candle at dusk,
when winter light steals away
earlier and earlier, and stars burn
colder each long night;

to fill the stockings on Christmas Eve
and then sit for a little while
in the colorful light of the trimmed tree,
sip an ounce of fine wine, slowly

and recall that all moments can be
occasions for harvest and joy,
ripe for some deed or insight;
to know at last that this slender moment
of idleness—my only life—is also right.

Leslie Schultz / Northfield, Minnesota

George Dila Memorial Flash Fiction Contest

Judged by Colleen Alles

Colleen Alles is a writer, former librarian & teacher, and Michigan girl for life. She earned her bachelor's degree in English from Michigan State University (2005) and her MLIS from Wayne State University (2015). Her fiction and poetry have appeared *in Red Cedar Review, Tar River Poetry, The Write Michigan Anthology, The Michigan Poet,* and other places. Her fiction has been long-listed for The Fugere Book Prize for Finely Crafted Novellas in 2023 (Regal House Publishing). Colleen is co-editor for fiction with *Barren Magazine* and is currently pursuing her MFA at Spalding University. Her house is chaotic with young children and a hound, so don't be shocked to encounter poems about chaotic houses, small children, or hounds.

Over a span of 3 months, Colleen read more than a hundred stories, narrowing them down to just 3 prize winners and 4 honorable mentions. Here they are along with Colleen's comments.

These stories are presented in no particular order. The three winning stories are not ranked 1,2,3. They are equal co-winning stories.

Winning Stories

***Dressed to Krill*:** by Sigrun Benjamin (Port Saint Lucie, Florida) This tale, cleverly rendered in present-tense sections and expertly written sentences, unfolds in an inevitable but deliciously satisfying way.

***Moirologist*:** by Colleen Addison (Bowen Island, British Columbia) I was immediately sitting up straight reading this highly atmospheric, ghostly meditation. Well-written and compelling; all the details are the right ones.

Blue Fever: by John Spudich (Berkeley, California) This straightforward story is quietly resonant, gently told, and resolves beautifully. I think the dialogue is particularly sweet, as are the images of constellations.

Honorable Mentions

Off the Menu: by JR Walsh (Oswego, New York). "Off the menu" alerts the reader to its humor early on and only gets funnier and more playful as it goes. I thought this was a treat, and clever to boot.

Reading Tea Leaves: by Elyse Ribbons (Lansing, Michigan). I love the premise of this story, and I love the twist! The details are evocative, the narrator quite inviting.

Hit Me With Your Best Shot: by Nan Jackson (East Lansing, Michign). I was drawn into this second-person romp immediately. The uncertainty and clipped sentences help this story achieve its chilly success.

A Queen Anne Treasure: by Kimberly Hayes (Chicago, Illinois).This engaging story is so much fun to read! The story starts strong and goes to unexpected places; I think it lands just right.

Dressed to Krill / Sigrun Benjamin

The boats go out at twilight, dressed in rust and hubris. We've long since traded nets for vacuum hoses sucking up the ocean's last flecks of silver. Krill: the new gold, the new god, the why not. We call it krilling, with that shrug we've perfected, the one that says, "What's a planet among friends?"

McDonald's still offers a krill burger, pink and chewy like a rubber glove. You can taste extinction in every bite. Feed the World, the flickering sign says, though the world is mostly water now, and the water is mostly hungry.

My mother krilled before me. Her boat was called The Last Laugh. Mine's The Bargain Bin. She taught me to name things ironically when the apocalypse gets chatty. She also taught me how to read the water's moods. "It remembers everything we did," she'd say. Her hands were calloused from hauling hoses slick with krill paste. She disappeared three years ago. The company called it an accident. I still have her captain's hat.

* * *

The whales remember.
That's what the riggers mutter under their salt and diesel breath. They say it's the blues, the humpbacks, the whales with their massive lungs taking the missing crews.

"They've developed a taste," Old Marlow says, spitting into his coffee.

"For what?" asks Denny, the new kid. First week on the water.

"For justice," Marlow replies.

We laugh, but not kindly. Laughter's a currency when the banks are all jellyfish.

* * *

The first blue I saw was a shadow beneath the boat, longer than sin.

"It's just a cloud," said Jax, my first mate, who always loved a good metaphor.

But clouds don't sing. Clouds don't have eyes that hold entire centuries of you did this.

Jax's hand found mine in the dark. We never spoke of it. Some terrors need to be private lest they become real.

* * *

We've turned the ocean into a soup kitchen. Salmon farms spread where forests once buzzed with cicadas. We feed the fish krill pellets, krill ash, and ash made of everything we've burned to power our world. The whales have to make do. So do we.

They used to teach kids that blues could swallow a car. Now they swallow trawlers.

No one believes it until their buddy's rig vanishes between swells. The company calls it "weather-related attrition." The paychecks still clear. The krill burgers still sizzle.

"They're getting smarter," Jax whispered one night, his face blue in the radar light. "They're hunting in formations now."

I told him to shut up and check the hoses.

* * *

Here's how it happens:

As you're pulling in a swarm, the hose starts shaking erratically until water flow ceases. The birds scatter first, because birds have the decency to panic. Then the deck tilts as if the ocean is inhaling. You see the mouth last. It's not a mouth, really. It's a cavernous maw tunnel lined with baleen, those keratinous curtains that once filtered unsuspecting prey. Now they filter you.

Whales don't chew. We're bite-sized to them, we're shrimp cocktail, we're krill in boots.

Three boats went missing last month. The company doubled our hazard pay. Nobody quit.

* * *

Jax disappeared on a Tuesday. One minute he was humming "Yellow Submarine," the next he was a dent in the fog. I called his name until my throat bled. The water swallowed the sound.

The company sent a card with a cartoon whale on it. Was it smiling? Sympathies for your loss! Beneath the exclamation point, someone had scribbled Apply for crew-replacement loans at...

I didn't cry. Crying's for when you still think the story's about you.

That night in my dream, Jax and my mother were playing cards inside a whale. "You're late," she said, dealing him in. I woke up laughing. Some jokes only make sense at the end of the world.

* * *

The whales are methodical. They've learned from us, see. They strike at shift changes, going for the engines first, because they know engines make us feel we're in charge.

At the docks, they've started selling whale insurance. Act now, get 10% off if you've been swallowed twice! The premiums are a joke. So's the deductible.

I've started to hear them at night. Breathing. Long, patient breaths under my ship's hull. Waiting.

* * *

My mother once told me that blues sing in dialects. Their songs delve into profound concepts that our simple minds cannot grasp. I wonder what they're singing now. A dirge? A dinner bell?

Last week, a rigger swore he heard them harmonizing with the krill pumps. "They're mocking us," he said, eyes wild.

"They're not," I told him. "Mocking requires malice. This is just ecology."

He quit the next day. Smart man.

* * *

Here's the secret they don't put on the krill-burger wrappers: We're the krill now.

Small. Swarming. Desperately trying to feed something that can't be fed.

The whales don't hate us. Hate is too specific. They're just… realigning the food chain. You don't need opposable thumbs to hold a grudge. Just time, teeth, and a memory longer than your own shadow.

I keep Jax's lighter in my pocket. Sometimes I flick it open just to see something that isn't blue or endless. The flame looks like hope, if you squint.

* * *

This morning, the water went quiet during my shift. Not a bird in sight. The hoses stopped shuddering.

I'm writing this in the belly of a boat that's not mine anymore. The hull groans like it's being crushed. The water is singing the familiar hymn, "Come home, come home."

They say blues can't digest steel. But they can digest the meat inside it.

When the mouth opens, I'll step into the baleen. Not brave. Not resigned. Just dressed to krill. I'll look for Jax. For my mother. For all of us who thought the ocean would keep giving forever.

Sigrun Benjamin / Port Saint Lucie, Florida

Blue Fever / John Spudich

She just didn't want to do it anymore. No more. No getting up in the sleepy blue coldness to milk the cow that lows and yearns. No sweeping up the long floorboards and beating at the rugs. No more sewing the rips in the overalls and the long johns stained with sweat. She didn't even enjoy now what she'd loved so recently, plucking the warm eggs from under the hens to hold them bright with life, there by the chicken coop where the sunflowers ravel.

He thought it was just a day or two, a minor bug she had caught or a poor night of sleep. But he began to grow worried as it dragged on and on. He would catch her looking off at nowhere, at the edge of the stiff green corn. He found her standing stock still at the butter churn, letting the cream sit cold and pearly like desert bones.

So he called in Doctor Langan who took some vitals at the wrist and temple, then listened to the dry rattle of her leaf-blown voice with the cold circle of his stethoscope. The doctor frowned with his great fleshy lugubrious jowls and pronounced that it was the Blue Fever. That's what people get in the big cities, Horace said, but the doctor told him no. It's an epidemic, eating everybody up, in the cities, in the country, in the one-horse towns. And it was unfortunately not a disease that responds to the tools at his disposal.

So Horace took Lottie in for a private meeting with Pastor Gentle. And after listening just a little bit, the Pastor spoke about the billowing smoke of the devil that blinds and the angels that spin down with charity and clarity to lay upon us their white-hot diamond hands. And many other soaring things from his fervent lips and his swelling chest. But Lottie, she looked through him, her eyes the color of the rusty blight that crawls up the husk of the corn. And later as she sat in the service, decked out fine in her Sunday yellow, there was no round sound in her hymnal, and her prayer dropped from the working of her lips as cold as river stones.

The tree witch was a little ride from town, living out there in an old cottage clotted with moss. She didn't react much to the diagnosis of Blue Fever, grunting lightly, then snapping her broad fingers for the cat to jump down, silky and long, from the examination table. She took Lottie's pulse in the neck, then in the wrist, listening head cocked sideways to the slightest warble of the hot beat. The witch looked at the lustrous whites of Lottie's eyes, and said to Horace that her health was sound. But then she told him: you must lie down with her this evening and look up at the ceiling together. Horace thanked her and gave her coin. He thought to ask some further question at the door, but when he turned to speak, the intensity of her black unblinking eyes arrested him, and soundlessly she looked up.

And so later that night Horace tried it. He lay with Lottie in the bed side by side. He looked up at the ceiling and so did she, and time passed for them. In the boredom and in the gloaming, he began to drift off, and he saw it open up above him, a night filled with stars. These were strange constellations, though, not the familiar shapes from his many nights on Earth. Lottie began to talk. It seemed she saw them too. He said to her, isn't that one strange, with the long tail? And she told him it was the Cockatrice, giver of birdsong, cereal, and plenitude. And then he asked about another, and she told him it was the Great Scalene, where justice and injustice are held in a perfectly unequal balance. Right next to the Apricot, and the Whistle just a little ways down. Though the brightest shape in the firmament was the Carriage House. And she unwound myths that spun from each, this one was lucky, that one spoke of the creation of haberdashery, while there was the image of the patron saint of deep sea divers and red-faced foxes. And the Wild Mulligan warned against the sins of impudence and condescension.

When they woke in the dim pre-dawn, they heard the heavy sound of the cow, with a moan like a moan of birthing. There was a strident urge to life within it that cared not for the hardy barreled tissue of its being. Horace said to her, last night was very interesting. And she said, thank you for coming to my night sky. And then Lottie swung out of bed with a light grunt and went to do her duty in the cold blue morning.

      John Spudich / Berkeley, California

Moirologist / Colleen Addison

During the recession I dyed my favorite cloak ebony, grew my hair long enough to rend, and hired out as a mourner. An only child with an absent father and long dead mother I had few other ways to make a living, and moirology seemed a good if temporary choice.

Paid to sob and dig my fingernails into half-circles on my palms, I watched choking on incense as coffin after coffin was lowered into the dirt underneath cemetery grass. I had missed my mother's rites so it was interesting at first, what with the dirges and the black cloths laid under candlesticks. Soon though I found paid mourning an art as nothing else.

I learned to wail harder when a eulogy struck an unrealistically too-kind note; to threaten a dive into the grave when after the service a lawyer announced a will-reading. I learned to recognize the reactions: the half-smothered relief, the shock, the way the bereaved walked across the floor as if expecting at any moment the tiles would crumble into insubstantiality. My fists were held up hopelessly to the sky when causes of death were mentioned, car accidents, cancer. I shook my cloak's fringes when family members appeared, faces frozen in a blank stare of grief.

The last funeral I attended was that of a woman. She had no lovers, few friends. She did have a child, who had been contacted but had been unable to come. I'd thought it would be easy, a final hurrah. Then the priest spoke. In the woman's house had been found poems, the pure beauty of them like sparkles over a dreary landscape. There were photos too: a garden tree, bare with winter; a brown bird feeding, small things but wonderful. A stray dog who had been fed howled and wouldn't stop howling.

The few neighbors blinked guilt-ridden and stunned at this eulogy. One began to cry, not prettily, great gulps rising out of the chest. I the absent child spread my cloak like wings trying to encompass all the sorrow. I widened my fingers.

Colleen Addison / Bowen Island, British Columbia

Off the Menu / JR Walsh

She asked if it was a good name. I didn't answer. We weren't talking about a dog or a cat. Or some shifty-eyed chameleon. This was the ongoing discussion. We'd been weighing every possible baby name for the past thirty-five months or years or so. Occasionally, we dabbled in months, days or flowers, but never fruit, and certainly not bakery items. Yet here she was, slapping two nouns together after the arrival of our newborn baby. Was she joking with me?

She doubled down. Asked if it was a good good one. Not if I liked the name, but if it were inherently good. Her forehead was active with worry, even though her entire body was exhausted from labor.

We'd made a definitive list of names that would gel with one or both of our last names should we choose to hyphenate. To my ear, this combo wouldn't harmonize with any surname on earth.

"What gives, hon?" I asked.

Various hospitals, invasive procedures, blood and more blood, miscarriages, rites of letting go, some giving up. She'd been through so much and this baby had too. She'd super-deep breathed her way through natural childbirth with only minimal scarification to my right palm and a quart or two of blood drawn from bite marks on my left shoulder.

"Don't hate me that I have to do this."

"Hate is a strong word and again, what gives?"

"Either I made a deal with the devil or with God," she said. "That if I survived, if she survived, we'd name her whatever they wanted."

"How do you know what they want?"

She appears to hold her breath. I'm sure that she can't explain, as if an explanation might wake the tiny baby on her chest.

I said, "But she can choose her own name later, right?"

"They are fine with that. I checked or... negotiated? It's never really clear where we stand."

"Just how in depth are your conversations with powerful good and/or evil spirits?"

She gestured like an expanding cloud around her head. I knew this to mean, her chats were all encompassing.

"Since I was a child. My father had them too," she said.

"Conversations."

"Conversations."

"But you've never mentioned it until now."

(In seven years exclamation point, though I kept that part to myself.)

I keep secrets too, like how I never took that ugly lamp to Goodwill because I think I can upcycle it. A slightly less ugly lamp could light up our baby's room when we read it stories, after all.

 "The voices kind of disappeared, or faded out when we started up," she said.

"You're welcome?"

"Then they came roaring back in pregnancy."

"You need sleep."

She nodded, closing her eyes. For all my resistance to the name, this baby did resemble a loaf of bread. A little blood balloon with flesh like water. She cried like a mother. A mother. She was hungry wet hair and disappearing fists. We were old and this was our last try. The labor seemed weeks long and no one slept for longer. No one died. Even my heart held. The midwives didn't need the ambulance around the corner. How would we deal with nothing wrong? Mother and baby slept with the same tight eyelashes.

Midwife Janice said, "Looks like you've got maybe 30 seconds and there's a birth certificate to sign. Follow me."
We approached the desk and she squinted at the paper. "It's not my place to judge."

"It's a much blessed and cursed family name," I said.

Was Midwife Janice hurrying me along? It had been a long day for her too, no doubt. Or is our baby a key to the Antichrist's takeover. Or is our baby the second coming of ... Stop it stop it stop it. I hadn't slept in 48 hours. I scribbled wherever it said signature. I felt a pinch in my heart and wondered if I should've checked one more time that this was indeed the name we were contractually bound to write on baseball gloves or tap shoes, but it was too late. The ink was dry and Midwife Janice said, "Good work, Pops!"

It felt good to know we were hyphenating anyway. This name is a lot a lot. Good good, I hope.

Ever since I was a child, I knew never to break an agreement with anyone with magic. Every fairy tale goes south in a hurry, if you betray a witch or talking animal. Break the promise and poof! The baby turns into dessert. Poof! The mother loses her ability to feel love. Poof! A monster eats them both. And then the townspeople shun me while I live forever with a broken heart and the shame of my shattered promises. In a cave, probably.

It was time to make the announcement calls. My phone had been melting out in the car. Scorching to the touch, the screen showed several missed texts and one in particular from a familiar unlisted number. It must be God or the Devil – they're always texting me some malarkey, though I never know which one it is. Today's text though is a miracle of emojis. Of course, they already knew! I probably don't need to text back, right? Should I send a thumbs up? I don't know if prayer hands would be offensive to at least one of them and/or possibly pandering to the other. What's the etiquette here?

                      JR Walsh / Oswego, New York

Reading Tea Leaves / Elyse Ribbons

I hadn't set out to read tea leaves for a living, but it quite literally fell into my lap. No, really, I was sitting at a teahouse in Old Town and someone knocked into my table and the tea spilled all over my lap.

But when I looked into my cup, the little bits and pieces of camellia sinensis swirled and tilted like a whirligig until suddenly, the shape of a perfect star formed. Within that star I saw a movement of black leather jackets and I was transported to a rock concert. I turned and saw a woman standing beside me with the brightest black eyes, like glowing obsidians and I knew that she was The One.

With a next blink I was back at the teahouse, the blonde who had knocked the table apologizing and trying to clean up. I asked her if she was going to a concert any time soon and she mentioned that she was headed to one later that evening. I told her that she would meet a woman with dark eyes and that she should ask for her number.

She gave me a weird look but smiled and shrugged it off. A week later I ran into her, and her new girlfriend, at the local farmer's market. So I began to explore this new talent, this new skill, and found that it lead to a very intriguing set of predictions and opportunities.

It's not always sunshine and lollipops, sadly, as there's a lot of tears, death and desperation in our futures as well. But certainly it helped me to make a few wise stock purchases so that most of my time can be spent reading books at teahouses.

I don't charge for my readings, that would be wrong, especially because sometimes I lie to people. Why ruin their night by warning them that their dog was going to be hit by a car? They couldn't stop it from happening, I'd learned the hard way that my predictions always came true.

Including the one that I am awaiting right now.

A crazed man, rabid with anger that the woman he'd abused for so many years had dared to leave him, had dared to dream of a life where she might be safe. But the thing is that she was going to be safe, after tonight.

I was no hero, I didn't want this to happen, but there's no avoiding your fate. So I sit here waiting for the blow, the final piercing sound of the gunshot. Which he wouldn't even intend on firing.

But he would slip on the tea that was about to spill at the girl's table. His head would crack open on the base of the large marble statue of Guanyin, the goddess of mercy. And he would be no more.

His gun, however, would go off when it hit the ground, his sweaty fingers still wrapped around the trigger. And then for me, it would be just blackness, like the darkest of lapsang souchongs. The fragrance of which still hung in the air, from the girl's spilled forth from the broken teapot and pooling on the floor, mingling with the blood.

   Elyse Ribbons / Lansing, Michigan

Hit Me With Your Best Shot / Nan Jackson

You don't know if it was before or after the wedding. In the basement of his parents' house in a small town in New England. Blasting Pat Benatar. Arms spread wide. Arms tucked close in a bear hug. Did you think you were alone? Did you think no-one could hear you? Up twirling. Down sweeping. Out of tune. Loud. The root-cellar tornado-shelter door to the outdoors shut at a slant.

It must have been before the wedding. Before the coffee and dessert reception in the dining room off the tiny kitchen in his parents' house. Before your aunt called on the land line from the west coast: Are you all married up now? You don't know how she got the number.

You know it was after he wrapped his hands around your throat. Fit of anger. Slut. That was in a different small town.

The night before the wedding you meet his friends downtown for Italian. He tells you to take communion when prompted by the priest tomorrow. You jump up, ask the waitress for the closest phone. In the back past the kitchen. Next to the emergency exit. White pages. Local listings. You call the minister of the Unitarian Universalist church. Would you have picked up the phone at 9 pm? She picks up the phone. Maybe an emergency.

It is an emergency. You ask her if it's okay. To take communion. The only church you ever attended was the UU. When you were a kid. Where you studied anthropology in a basement classroom. Where you were allowed into the main hall at Easter to trade flower bouquets. You'd walk up the aisle, bring your handful of flowers to the stage. Maybe it wasn't Easter. The peonies were in bloom. Lush and pungent and covered with ants. May Day?

You hold the black Bakelite receiver tight to your ear. Stretch the coil as far as it will go. The minister says something you barely hear above the din of the restaurant. The clang of pots and pans. Laughter from the bar. Did she really say It's Up To You?

Morning comes. You walk up the aisle holding a bouquet, the flowers magnifying the ever-so-slight shaking in your hands. You loosen your grip. Say the words. Take communion. You travel home to the different small town. You think you're happy. He waits a few months. Takes revenge.

    Nan Jackson / East Lansing, Michigan

A Queen Anne Treasure / Kimberly Hayes

I padded into the bathroom. I wanted a cigarette, but I wasn't in the mood to get dressed for a smoke. From the doorway, I glanced back at the bedroom. We met a few hours ago on a blind date. After we spent the night dancing and drinking, he was now passed out, snoring. It was time to go home. I decided to leave before things became uncomfortable.

He lived in an old house he'd been restoring for the past few years. Seeing it from the inside was a treat—it was one of my favorite houses in the area. He had given me a grand tour before we tumbled into bed.

The house was Queen Anne style, built in the early 1900s. Details within the woodwork, flooring, and fireplace mantels were unbelievable. He was doing an amazing job, and I couldn't wait to see what it would look like when he finished.

I took a scalding hot shower, letting the bathroom fog until I couldn't see. It was heaven to stand and let the hot water beat down on me for a bit.

As the steam faded away, I stared into the mirror over the sink and watched with curiosity as a message appeared.

Start searching now. There is money hidden around the house.

I looked around the bathroom. I peeked into the bedroom. My date from last night was still sleeping. Was there a camera hidden somewhere?

"Is this a joke or set up for a TV show? How do you know this? Are you a ghost?" I whispered, not wanting to wake him up.

The mirror clouded over, and another message materialized.

This is not a joke. The previous owner stashed money all over the house. Some places are easier to find than others. A few you might have to work at accessing. Go look. I will guide you.

"Why are you telling me this? Where do I start?"

The mirror fogged up again.

"Get dressed and start in the basement. I will guide you. My name is Elizabeth."

As I grabbed my clothes, my date stirred in the bed. I put on my clothes from the night before in the living room and found the steps to the basement.

The basement was unfinished, but it was clean. A faint female voice spoke up. In the corner, by the back door. That bookshelf hides an envelope.

I looked around, but didn't see anyone. "Elizabeth? Who are you?"

"I am the wife of the farmer who built this house. We raised our family here. I died after falling down the steps and breaking my neck. The bookshelf, the envelope should be towards the bottom."

As I searched through the bookshelf, I asked Elizabeth why money was hidden all over the house.

"The previous owner didn't trust banks. His children thought he was unstable and tried to force him to leave, but he refused."

I found the envelope stashed between two encyclopedias. It was yellow with age and taped up well.

"Look in the crawl space under the stairs. There should be another envelope."

"Why are you telling me this? How did you find out where all this money is hidden?" I whispered.

"My husband grieved for me before moving away. I'm unable to leave. I have become a guardian, if you will, of the house. I watched the previous owner hide his money during the time he lived here."

I let that sink in before asking, "Is my date from last night aware of you? Does he know about the money stashes?"

"He has heard rumors. I do not know whether he knows the full history of the house or is aware of my existence. I've never made myself known to him. I suspect the previous owner was aware of me, but he was mentally unstable; he didn't trust banks."

Elizabeth guided me elsewhere in the basement, to a loose floorboard in the kitchen, then to a small closet in the hallway. That one I had to stand on tiptoe to reach. Each one had a sealed, business-size envelope. Each one was bulging with what I guessed was cash.

The final envelope was behind a loose upstairs baseboard in another bedroom. Elizabeth said there was more, but my lover from the night before was stirring. I thanked her and let myself out the back door. The money was heavy in my purse. I wondered how much I had found and what was still in the house.

Lighting a much-needed cigarette, I ordered an Uber and started looking up any history of the house that I hadn't already read about.

There was a lot out there via newspaper articles, neighborhood associations, even Wikipedia, including more about the previous owner. As Elizabeth had said, he never trusted banks, and after his wife passed away, his mental state turned to mush. He never told his children that he hid money anywhere. From one of the articles I found, they were upset he didn't leave them anything but the house. They sold the house and split the money earned from the sale.

Elizabeth's husband built the house around the turn of the previous century. He raised his family there and lived to be one hundred years old. Elizabeth died in her sixties after slipping and falling down the stairs. None of the articles I read mentioned that her spirit lingered in the house. My date from last night didn't know about her. I wondered why she was unable to leave.

I double-checked the money to confirm the amount. It was enough for me to do whatever I wanted for the rest of my life. I knew then that I wanted to buy the house from my lover and finish what he had started.

    Kimberly Hayes / Chicago, Illinois

Lifted / Emily Zhang

Charcoal Drawing
Emily Zhang / Bellevue, Washington

Made in the USA
Middletown, DE
09 September 2025

12943138R00038